# TOGETHER

## Strong in Spirit

By Sarah Brooks, Sophie Danielson &
Nancy Lindgren

A mentoring guide for children
& their mentors

# ENDORSEMENTS

"I think you have hit a home run with this children's guide! The sessions provide just the right amount of material for mentees to remain interested and for mentors to tailor it to the age and maturity of the child. God bless you for caring about children growing in the knowledge of the Lord!"

**Marilynn Rarick**
**Mentor**

"**Together: Strong in Spirit** is a great tool for adults to teach kids about the character of God. In each session, kids will have the opportunity to connect emotionally before they connect spiritually with their mentor. I love that the guide includes coloring activities to help kinesthetic learners engage with the material. If your hope is to have a mentoring relationship with a kid, start here!"

**Lisa Youngstrand**
**Mother & Mentor**

"Thank you for all of your hard work in designing this mentoring guide for children! The overall purpose is excellent. I love where your hearts are for mentoring our young people and found value in using this guide."

**Phyl Burger**
**Mentor**

"I loved going through the prayer guide with my granddaughter. It made her more comfortable in praying out loud. We loved the coloring pages. We met in person one time and by Zoom the other times. It was so sweet to color in person with her. This is a great way to build relationships and share our faith. Thank you so much for this guide and all the other guides which are so helpful in building relationships."

**Shelley Sadler**
**Grandmother & Mentor**

"I have several favorite things about this guide, including the nervous caterpillar in the 'God Is With Me' coloring page! I really appreciated the 'How To Use This Guide' at the beginning—the tone set here is actually incredible. The way that the mentors are empowered to do their best, to show up as themselves, to use the guide for what it is and not be bound to it, and to have reminders of what is impactful in the mentor's life is so good. I also see the great value of Scripture. It's important to lean on Scripture so I appreciate that this is the case in this guide. I love how this guide personalizes Scripture by putting our own name into the verse. It's a really wonderful guide and I hope the framework will create great relationships and lay great foundations for kids growing into great and faithful adults."

**Travis Moore**
**Mentor**

“I didn’t know when God laid it on my heart to ask someone to be my mentor that it would set in motion a desire for my young daughter to tell me that she wanted to begin praying for her own mentor. We prayed and God brought someone into her life when she was 13. Oh how I would have loved a children’s mentoring guide like this when she was younger. I believe I would have found a mentor sooner if I had a guide like this to equip a mentor. Mentoring is sometimes viewed as an adult experience. I’m here to tell you the desire in our little ones is strong for connection and truth. Anyone who loves Jesus will be equipped as every detail in this guide is laid out so beautifully with so much wiggle room to fit the needs of the child. It is never too early to guide them in understanding who God is and how we can know Him better through the power and discipline of our prayers. This is an inspiring guide full of wisdom, teaching our children the importance of understanding God’s character and seeking Him in prayer so that their faith can begin to build deep, immovable roots.”

**Jeannine Mitchell**
**Mother & Mentor**

“Wow! I am so excited for this guidebook. As someone who has always been hesitant to step into teaching roles for kiddos, this guidebook allows for grace, offers unending encouragement and countless resources. It is a super solid guidebook on how to mentor our littles into knowing the Lord deeper and better while also growing our own understanding and deepening our faith. We are going to raise a generation of kids that will grow up feeling seen and heard, and knowing they are loved by the God of the universe. I am excited to have this as a resource as my children grow, as well as offer this to other parents and mentors as a resource.”

**Kaity Van Dyke**
**Mother & Mentor**

Illustrated by Kole Kostelic.


A MORE Mentoring resource in alliance with MORE Mentoring.

ISBN: 979-8-9865529-9-6

# This book belongs to:

Birthday:

Favorite color:

Family members:

I feel loved when:

# Table of Contents

# HOW TO USE THIS GUIDE
## A note for mentors

Hey Mentor! You are awesome! We hope you know that. Thank you for your willingness to step into a mentoring relationship with a child—whether you are a parent, grandparent, teacher, relative or just an amazing human who cares about mentoring our next generation. We have prayed for you, and with confidence in the Lord we know you and your mentee's life will be greatly impacted.

As a mom of five, I (Sarah) understand the great juggling act of time, capacity, and resources. This guide is designed to be "open and go" so you don't have to plan ahead. We encourage you to show up ready, mindfully, and prayerfully to connect with God and each other. The following tips show you how to use this guide to its full potential.

**GLANCE AHEAD -** Take a glance at the next session, then be prepared for conversation and questions. A preview of the session will give you an idea of the topic and help you decide how much you want to do that day. You can decide which questions you want to ask and whether to utilize the appendix packed with activities, questions, topics, and Scripture.

**GO AT YOUR OWN PACE -** This guide is designed to be a fun tool for engagement, deeper connection, and prayer. We don't want you to ever feel rushed or frustrated! If you prefer to skip a question, do that. And if you sense the child is done, stop and return to the session another day. If it takes you a few meeting times to go through one session, that is perfectly fine!

**MEETING TOGETHER -** This is up to you! You can meet at home, out at a favorite place, or video chat for those who live far away. You can meet after school, on Saturday morning, before bed . . . you pick what's best! And how often is also up to you; but remember, the more consistently you meet with your mentee (every week or every two), the more your mentoring will have an impact.

**GETTING TO KNOW YOU -** Questions are a huge part of a healthy mentoring relationship. We have provided questions for each session for you to ask one another. Plus, there are additional questions in the back, designed especially for the older mentees in mind. Feel free to ask all the questions or just a couple. Stay curious. Each session includes a prompt, "Today, I'm feeling . . ." with corresponding cartoons. This feature is intended to spark conversation about our emotions.

**ENCOURAGEMENT FOR YOU –** This book helps equip you to enter a mentoring relationship. You don't need to have all the answers or know exactly what you are doing. Leave perfection at the door and bring wonderful, amazing YOU. We have provided Scripture and resources for those big questions that might be asked. And we encourage you to stay in the questioning/listening zone as you work through different topics or moments. Most importantly, take it all to Jesus in prayer together! He is where all the true answers can be found.

**STRONG IN SPIRIT –** This is the opportunity to learn more about who the Holy Spirit is and how the Fruit of the Spirit works. Press into the verses, questions, and simple lessons provided. Feel free to use the appendix to further the conversation or take it straight to prayer.

**PRAYER – LOOK WITH THE EYES OF YOUR HEART**

Prayer is one of the most beautiful and important parts of the mentoring experience. The power of prayer is real, and there's nothing more beautiful than teaching a child how to pray and then listening to him or her talk to God.

> *Do not be anxious about anything, but in every situation, by prayer and petition, with thanksgiving, present your requests to God. And the peace of God, which transcends all understanding, will guard your hearts and your minds in Christ Jesus* (Philippians 4:6–7).

Prayer is where our burdens are lifted as our focus shifts from our circumstances to our great God. When our hearts unite with another and we agree in faith for God's best plan, it changes us. We move from fear to trust, from worry to rest, from doubt to hope, and from anxiety to peace. Prayer ultimately draws us closer to the Lord and to others.

And prayer is just as much about listening as it is talking. The Lord wants to speak to us. Take the time to be silent and listen for His voice, modeling for your child the beautiful aspect of listening as well as asking in prayer. Sometimes, though, we or the child may feel shy or not know what to say. The **Prayer Prompts** in each session provide direction and inspiration for being intentional about prayer. It's important to remember that prayer is not about saying the "right words." Prayer is the posture of your heart that draws you into sweeter intimacy and a deeper relationship with the Lord.

*I keep asking that the God of our Lord Jesus Christ, the glorious Father, may give you the Spirit of wisdom and revelation, so that you may know him better. I pray that the eyes of your heart may be enlightened in order that you may know the hope to which he has called you* (Ephesians 1:17–18a).

We are teaching these little ones to pray using the eyes of their heart—to Look:

**Look Up - God, I love You**
This exercise teaches children to look up at God—the posture of praise. Together with your mentee, look at the heart of God, His attributes, and His character. Then praise Him for who He is. When we start with a focus on God, He becomes greater and our circumstances become much smaller. Praise also defeats the enemy. This book includes example sentences to guide you in praise, but feel free to adjust them to best help you show your mentee what it looks like to praise God!

**Look Within - God, I am sorry**
We have all fallen short and we want children to know this too. We are healed and cleansed when we bring our sin and mistakes to God. Confession frees us to move forward in repentance to become all God has created us to be. And there is something beautiful when a child hears us adults admit we sinned and to say we are sorry.

**Look Around - Thank You, God**
It's really hard for our hearts to feel sad or scared when we are thankful. This is our opportunity to model and help children to show gratitude. Take turns telling God what you are thankful for, and watch gratitude impact your mentee's life as he or she gives thanks to the ultimate giver.

**Look To Him - Help me, God**
The Bible tells us to ask God to meet our needs, as He is the provider. What a beautiful thing for a child to learn early on—instead of going to the internet or to their own knowledge or skills, to stop and ask God first.

**COLORING PAGES -** Each session includes a fun coloring activity. One side highlights the topic of each session and a characteristic of God. The other side includes the main Bible verse that can be hung up or memorized. We suggest playing music as you color together, engage in activities and memorize Scripture. Get creative with different music, especially songs that highlight the Fruit of the Spirit and the characteristics of God. Music is a great way to worship and connect to God and to each other!

**VERSES -** Every session will include a main verse to connect with God through Scripture, and it is located in the prayer section as well as the coloring page. We want to expose our younger mentees to Scripture, but we also want them to know they can show up just as they are. We don't necessarily encourage any homework, nor do we want to make this a "should" or "have to." You are always welcome to create a way for them to connect with God through Scripture to help keep these powerful verses in their minds.

> **Ideas -** Write the verse down and hang it up, mark it in their Bible, review the verses when you meet, memorize each verse for little prizes, create motions, songs or chants to better remember, or simply read the Scripture and ask questions about it!

**APPENDIX -** We'd be lying if we said we weren't excited for this section! Take a look in the back for helpful resources to connect with God and your child on an even deeper level.

> **Scripture -** Additional Scripture for each session. We have provided more Scriptures that talk about God's love, joy, peace, patience, kindness, goodness, faithfulness, gentleness and self-control.
>
> **Dive Deeper -** This section is for you and your mentee to dive a little deeper if you have the time and/or if your mentee has questions.
>
> **Getting to Know You -** Additional conversation starter questions for your mentee.
>
> **Activity Recommendations -** This is for those who want to extend the session and get more hands-on with crafts and activities that connect to the teaching.
>
> **Leading a Mentee to Christ -** We offer this prayer for you to guide your mentee if they want to accept Christ as their Savior.
>
> **Emotion Wheel -** We've also added emotion wheels for boys and girls at the back of the book to encourage further discussion about our feelings.

# SESSION one

**SESSION 1**

HOLY SPIRIT - GOD IS MY **HELPER** **DATE** ____________

# GETTING TO KNOW **YOU**

If you could be any character from a story or a movie, who would you want to be?

Would you rather be able to speak to animals or speak all the languages in the world?

What do you know about the Holy Spirit?

What does the word "truth" mean to you?

These questions are meant to kickstart the conversation. You don't need to ask all of them—let the discussion naturally guide you based on the flow with your mentee.

# TODAY
## I'M FEELING . . .

excited

hopeful

worried

frustrated

creative

joyful

confused

**What are you curious about today?**

# GOD IS MY HELPER

When Jesus left the earth and went to be with God, He left His Spirit for us so that He can be with us.

Who is the Holy Spirit? What does He do?

The Holy Spirit is our **HELPER.**

He reminds us of Bible verses and truths about God.

He is kind, giving, helps us obey, teaches us, guides us, keeps us safe and helps us be more like Jesus.

He often speaks to us through Scripture, people, songs, dreams, things you see or experience, circumstances, and sometimes a feeling in your heart.

Do you have the Holy Spirit in you?

What questions do you have about the Holy Spirit?

You can dive deeper into this topic in the Appendix. Page 103 includes additional Scripture about the Holy Spirit and page 120 can help you lead a mentee to Christ.

See **Appendix** for more verses.

## Let's pray together!

### Look Up to Him in Praise – God, I love that You are my **Helper.**

*But the Helper, the Holy Spirit, whom the Father will send in my name, he will teach you all things and bring to your remembrance all that I have said to you* (John 14:26, ESV).

### Look Within and Say I am Sorry – God, I am sorry . . .

We all make mistakes and God asks us to come to Him and tell Him so He can help us and we can say I am sorry. This makes our hearts clean and happy.

### Look Around and Thank Him – God, thank You for . . .

What are you thankful for today?
Remember, when we are thankful, it's hard for our hearts to feel sad or afraid.

### Look to Him and Ask – God, be my **Helper.**

What is something you need God to help you with or something you want to ask Him for?

Now we are going to do something fun! We are going to put your name in this verse as we pray because we are praying God's will and His heart for us.

*And I will ask the Father, and he will give* _______________ *another Helper, to be with* _____________ *forever, even the Spirit of truth, whom the world cannot receive because it neither sees him nor knows him.* ______________ *knows him, for he dwells with* ____________ *and will be in* ____________ (John 14:16–17, ESV).

GOD IS MY HELPER

"But the Helper, the Holy Spirit, whom the Father will send in my name, he will teach you all things and bring to your remembrance all that I have said to you."

John 14:26 (ESV)

# JOURNAL
## Prompt

Anxiety and radical gratitude cannot coexist! Help your mentee choose gratitude by encouraging them to journal things they are grateful for beyond the surface level stuff. This can be hard to do. You are welcome to model it for them.

Today, I am grateful for . . .

## Today, I am praying for . . .

*"This [gratitude journal section] is maybe one of the single most impactful things I've implemented in my life. My wife and I tell each other at least three things we're grateful for from the day as we go to bed. We've been doing that for six years now and it completely changes the way we feel and think. Building that practice into a child can lay a great foundation for how they see the world and how they navigate and cope with hard realities."*

**Travis Moore**
**Mentor**

# SESSION two

SESSION 2

FRUIT OF THE SPIRIT - GOD IS **WITH ME** **DATE** ______________

# GETTING TO KNOW **YOU**

If you could visit anywhere in the world, where would it be?

If you could choose only one fruit to eat for the rest of your life, which one would you choose? Why?

Do you have any questions or thoughts about the Holy Spirit?

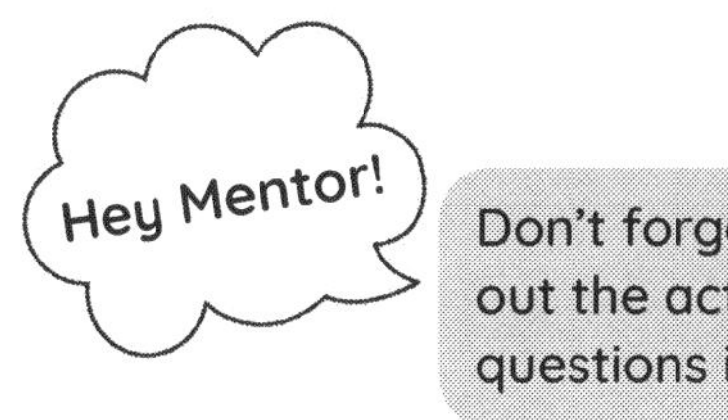


Don't forget to check out the activities and questions in the back!

# **TODAY** I'M FEELING . . .

excited

hopeful

worried

frustrated

creative

joyful

confused

**What are you curious about today?**

# GOD IS WITH ME

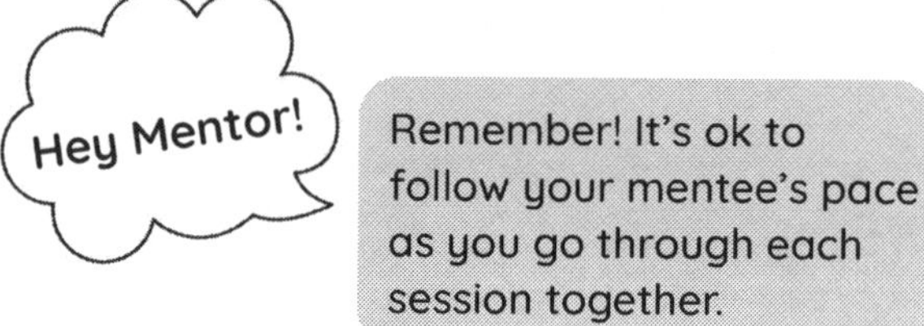


Galatians 5:23 says:
*But the fruit of the Spirit is love, joy, peace, patience, kindness, goodness, faithfulness, gentleness and self-control.*

Where does yummy, juicy fruit come from and what does fruit need to grow? (Possible answers: soil, sun, water, connected to the branch)

YES! We know delicious ripe fruit comes from happy plants and trees that have good soil and receive the right amount of sunlight and rain.

Would the fruit still grow if it wasn't connected to the tree?

Fruit needs to be connected to the branch and connected to the tree to grow.

Just like fruit grows, we grow and produce fruit when we stay connected to God and to the Holy Spirit. Not like the fruit that we eat, but the **FRUIT** of the Spirit. We experience HIS love, joy, peace, patience, kindness, goodness, faithfulness, gentleness and self-control and live it out every day.

He makes us grow. When we remain in Him, (that means to say yes to Him and remain close), WE produce fruit.

I can't wait to learn more about the Fruit of the Spirit with you!

See **Appendix** for more activities.

## Let's pray together!

### Look Up to Him in Praise – God, I love that You are **with me** always.

*So do not fear, for I am with you; do not be dismayed, for I am your God. I will strengthen you and help you; I will uphold you with my righteous right hand* (Isaiah 41:10).

### Look Within and Say I am Sorry – God, I am sorry . . .

We all sin and God asks us to come to Him and tell Him so He can help us and we can say I am sorry. This makes our hearts clean and happy.

### Look Around and Thank Him – God, thank You for . . .

What are you thankful for today?
Remember, when we are thankful, it's hard for our hearts to feel sad or afraid.

### Look to Him and Ask – God, help me to be **brave.**

What is something you need God to help you with or something you want to ask Him for?

Now we are going to do something fun! We are going to put your name in this verse as we pray because we are praying God's will and His heart for us.

*Be strong and courageous. Do not be afraid or terrified because of them, for the LORD your God goes with ____________; he will never leave ____________ nor forsake you* (Deuteronomy 31:6).

GOD IS WITH ME

**“Fear not, for I am with you; be not dismayed, for I am your God; I will strengthen you, I will help you, I will uphold you with my righteous right hand.”**

Isaiah 41:10 (ESV)

# JOURNAL
## Prompt

Today, I am grateful for . . .

Today, I am praying for . . .

# SESSION three

**SESSION 3**

LOVE - GOD IS **LOVE**

**DATE** ______________________

We recommend reviewing the "How to use this guide" pages to be reminded and get excited for your session!

# GETTING TO KNOW **YOU**

What's the best thing you've ever built or created, and what was it made of?

Would you rather live in a treehouse or a castle?

Who is someone you love a lot?

Who is someone in your life who needs love?

See the **Appendix** for more questions.

# **TODAY** I'M FEELING . . .

excited

hopeful

worried

frustrated

creative

joyful

confused

**What are you curious about today?**

# GOD IS LOVE

Galatians 5:23 says:
*But the fruit of the Spirit is love, joy, peace, patience, kindness, goodness, faithfulness, gentleness and self-control.*

The Fruit of the Spirit are characteristics of God. We are close to God and have Him in our hearts, which makes us more like Him.

Did you see what the first fruit is? It's LOVE and that is because God IS love. God loves you so much. He loves you and me more than we can even imagine. He NEVER stops loving us, and He wants to fill us with His deep, great love.

Pretend you are a giant bucket (hold your hands out in front of you in a circle like you're making a bucket) and that God is pouring out His love into you.

Guess what—that bucket would be spilling over because God has SO much love for you. You know what else?

God thinks you are pretty great and really special. He wants His love for you to spill out and spill onto others.

Our world needs so much love and YOU and I get to give God's love to others. Let's think of some ways we can show love to the people around us—like our neighbors, our family, or friends and teachers at school.

See **Appendix** for more verses.

## Let's pray together!

### Look Up to Him in Praise – God, I love that You are **Love.**

*And so we know and rely on the love God has for us. God is love. Whoever lives in love lives in God, and God in them* (1 John 4:16).

### Look Within and Say I am Sorry – God, I am sorry . . .

We all make mistakes and God asks us to come to Him and tell Him so He can help us and we can say I am sorry. This makes our hearts clean and happy.

### Look Around and Thank Him – God, thank You for . . .

What are you thankful for today?
Remember, when we are thankful, it's hard for our hearts to feel sad or afraid.

### Look to Him and Ask – God, help me to **Love others.**

What is something you need God to help you with or something you want to ask Him for?

Now we are going to do something fun! We are going to put your name in this verse as we pray because we are praying God's will and His heart for us.

*A new command I give ______________: Love one another. As I have loved ______________, so you must love one another. By this everyone will know that ______________ [is] my disciple, if you love one another* (John 13:34–35).

GOD IS LOVE

**"So we have come to know and to believe the love that God has for us. God is love, and whoever abides in love abides in God, and God abides in him."**

1 John 4:16 (ESV)

# JOURNAL
## Prompt

Today, I am grateful for . . .

## Today, I am praying for . . .

# SESSION four

**SESSION 4**

LOVE - GOD IS **JOY** **DATE** ____________________

## GETTING TO KNOW
# YOU

---

What's the funniest thing you've ever read in a book or story?

If you could invent a new ice cream flavor, what would it be and what would you name it?

How do you share joy with others around you?

Can you think of a time when you felt joy even when things were difficult? What helped you feel that way?

---

See the **Appendix** for more questions.

# TODAY
## I'M FEELING . . .

excited

hopeful

worried

frustrated

creative

joyful

confused

**What are you curious about today?**

# GOD IS JOY

Galatians 5:23 says:
*But the fruit of the Spirit is love, joy, peace, patience, kindness, goodness, faithfulness, gentleness and self-control.*

What makes you so very happy? (Christmas morning, first day of summer, swimming, popsicles, trips...)

I feel so joyful when ____.

But you know what? Sometimes, I don't feel very joyful.

Sometimes I feel worried, sad, nervous or angry. Those emotions are all normal, but here is what is true. Did you know that we can feel God's joy even when we are sad?

Nehemiah 8:10b says:
*Do not grieve, for the joy of the Lord is your strength.*

God is **joy** and He gives us His **joy** even when we feel nervous or angry. In fact, it is HIS **joy** that helps us work through all of those things.

He comforts us and helps us, and when our hearts turn to Him for help, when we feel sad or afraid, we can also experience His joy. That may seem weird or strange, so let's pray and talk to God and ask Him about it.

## Let's pray together!

### Look Up to Him in Praise – God, I love that You are **Joy.**

*I have told you this so that my joy may be in you and that your joy may be complete* (John 15:11).

### Look Within and Say I am Sorry – God, I am sorry . . .

We all mess up sometimes, and God wants us to come to Him and admit it. When we say sorry to God, He helps us feel better and makes our hearts clean and happy.

### Look Around and Thank Him – God, thank You . . .

What are you thankful for today?
Thanking God helps us experience His joy!

### Look to Him and Ask – God, fill me with Your **Joy**!

*May the God of hope fill ____________ with all joy and peace as ____________ trust(s) in him, so that ____________ may overflow with hope by the power of the Holy Spirit* (Romans 15:13).

GOD IS JOY

**"I have told you this so that my joy may be in you and that your joy may be complete."**

John 15:11

# JOURNAL
## Prompt

Today, I am grateful for . . .

Today, I am praying for . . .

# SESSION five

**SESSION 5**

PEACE – GOD IS **PEACE**

**DATE** ____________________

## GETTING TO KNOW **YOU**

If you could design your own playground, what would it look like?

If you could time travel, would you go to the past or the future? What would you do there?

What does peace mean to you, and how does it make you feel?

Can you remember a time when you felt really calm and peaceful? What was happening?

See the **Appendix** for more questions.

## **TODAY** I'M FEELING . . .

excited

hopeful

worried

frustrated

creative

joyful

confused

**What are you curious about today?**

# GOD IS PEACE

Galatians 5:23 says:
*But the fruit of the Spirit is love, joy, peace, patience, kindness, goodness, faithfulness, gentleness and self-control.*

Have you ever felt worried or scared about something? Maybe it's a big test at school, a disagreement with a friend, or just feeling unsure about things. Jesus understands how you feel, and He has something very special to tell you about peace.

In John 14:27, Jesus says:
*"Peace I leave with you; my peace I give you. I do not give to you as the world gives. Do not let your hearts be troubled and do not be afraid."*

What does this mean? Jesus is saying that He wants to give us a special kind of peace. This peace is different from what we might find in the world. It's not just about being calm or quiet. It's a deep, comforting peace that comes from knowing that Jesus is always with us and that He loves us no matter what.

When we have Jesus' peace, we can feel calm even when things around us are a bit crazy. We don't have to be afraid because we know that Jesus is taking care of us. So, whenever you feel worried or afraid, remember that Jesus is with you and He wants to fill your heart with His amazing peace.

You can talk to Him anytime and ask Him to help you feel His peace. Just close your eyes, take a deep breath, and say, "Jesus, please give me Your peace." He loves you so much and wants you to feel safe and loved.

So, let's trust in Jesus and keep our hearts full of His wonderful peace!

## Let's pray together!

**Look Up to Him in Praise** – God, I love that You are **Peace.**

*Peace I leave with you; my peace I give you. I do not give to you as the world gives. Do not let your hearts be troubled and do not be afraid* (John 14:27).

**Look Within and Say I am Sorry** – God, I am sorry . . .

We all mess up sometimes, and God wants us to come to Him and admit it. When we say sorry to God, He helps us feel better and makes our hearts clean and happy.

**Look Around and Thank Him** – God, thank You for Your **Peace** . . .

What are you thankful for today?

When we are thankful, it's hard for our hearts to feel worried or anxious. Thanking God helps us experience His peace.

**Look to Him and Ask** – God, give me Your **Peace**.

*Do not be anxious, ______________ , about anything, but in every situation, by prayer and petition, with thanksgiving, present your requests to God. And the peace of God, which transcends all understanding, will guard ______________ ('s) heart and ______________ ('s) mind in Christ Jesus* (Philippians 4:6–7).

GOD IS PEACE

"Peace I leave with you; my peace I give you. I do not give to you as the world gives. Do not let your hearts be troubled and do not be afraid."

John 14:27

# JOURNAL
## Prompt

Today, I am grateful for . . .

# Today, I am praying for . . .

# SESSION six

**SESSION 6**

PATIENCE – GOD IS **PATIENT** **DATE** ______________________

## GETTING TO KNOW **YOU**

If you could create a new holiday, what would it be called and how would people celebrate it?

What's your favorite kind of weather and what do you like to do when it's that weather?

What do you think it means to have patience?

How can practicing patience help you show God's love to others?

See the **Appendix** for more questions.

## **TODAY** I'M FEELING . . .

excited

hopeful

worried

frustrated

creative

joyful

confused

**What are you curious about today?**

# GOD IS PATIENT

Galatians 5:23 says:
*But the fruit of the Spirit is love, joy, peace, patience, kindness, goodness, faithfulness, gentleness and self-control.*

Do you know what can be super boring? Road trips! It's so hard being in the car for a long time. Have you taken a road trip? Where did you go? Was it hard as you waited to get there?

**Patience** can be really hard, especially when we're waiting for something exciting or when things aren't going our way.

But did you know that **patience** is something God wants to help us with? Did you know **patience** actually makes us STRONGER?

Colossians 1:9b–11 says:
*We continually ask God to fill you with the knowledge of his will through all the wisdom and understanding that the Spirit gives, so that you may live a life worthy of the Lord and please him in every way: bearing fruit in every good work, growing in the knowledge of God, being strengthened with all power according to his glorious might so that you may have great endurance and patience . . .*

God gives us strength to be **patient** and keep going, even when it's tough. Being **patient** helps us to live in a way that makes us depend on God and helps us grow closer to Him.

So, next time you feel impatient, remember that God is with you, giving you the strength to wait. Trust Him, and He will help you be **patient** and strong!

## Let's pray together!

### Look Up to Him in Praise – God, I love that You are **Patient.**

*This means that, contrary to man's perspective, the Lord is not late with his promise to return, as some measure lateness. But rather, his "delay" simply reveals his loving patience toward you, because he does not want any to perish but all to come to repentance* (2 Peter 3:9, TPT).

### Look Within and Say I am Sorry – God, I am sorry . . .

We all sin, and God wants us to come to Him and admit it. Was there a time recently that you were not patient? Let's talk to God about it.

### Look Around and Thank Him – God, thank You for . . .

What are you thankful for today?
When we are thankful, it's hard for our hearts to feel impatient or grumpy. Thanking God helps us experience His patience.

### Look to Him and Ask – God, help me be **Patient.**

*So that _______________ may live a life worthy of the Lord and please him in every way: bearing fruit in every good work, growing in the knowledge of God, being strengthened with all power according to his glorious might so that _______________ may have great endurance and patience* (Colossians 1:10–11).

GOD IS PATIENT

"This means that, contrary to man's perspective, the Lord is not late with his promise to return, as some measure lateness. But rather, his 'delay' simply reveals his loving patience toward you, because he does not want any to perish but all to come to repentance."

2 Peter 3:9 (TPT)

# JOURNAL
## Prompt

Today, I am grateful for . . .

## Today, I am praying for . . .

# SESSION seven

**SESSION 7**
KINDNESS – GOD IS **KIND**

**DATE** ____________

## GETTING TO KNOW **YOU**

What's your favorite snack to eat after school?

If you could have a party with any theme, what theme would you choose?

Can you share a time when someone was kind to you? How did it make you feel?

How does God show kindness to us, and how can we share that kindness with others?

See the **Appendix** for more questions.

## **TODAY** I'M FEELING . . .

excited

hopeful

worried

frustrated

creative

joyful

confused

**What are you curious about today?**

# GOD IS KING

Galatians 5:23 says:
*But the fruit of the Spirit is love, joy, peace, patience, kindness, goodness, faithfulness, gentleness and self-control.*

Have you ever been afraid of the dark? I know I don't always love it when it's dark and when I can't see.

Do you know what kindness is like? Kindness is like a nightlight shining in a dark room. Kindness is a little light that makes the world a brighter and happier place. The Bible tells us a lot about kindness and how important it is to be kind to others.

In Titus 3:4–5 (MSG), it says:
*But when God, our kind and loving Savior God, stepped in, he saved us from all that. It was all his doing; we had nothing to do with it. He gave us a good bath, and we came out of it new people, washed inside and out by the Holy Spirit.*

Did it make you laugh when it said, "He gave us a good bath?" It's silly, but so true! We are a mess, and yet, God showed us the greatest kindness by saving us and making us clean. He did this because He loves us so much.

Just like God shows us kindness, we can show kindness to others too. What are some ways you can be kind to your siblings, friends or family? (help a friend, share our toys, say kind words, or give a big smile . . .)

Every act of kindness, no matter how small, makes a big difference just like a little nightlight in a dark room.

## Let's pray together!

### Look Up to Him in Praise – God, I love that You are **Kind.**

*I will tell of the kindnesses of the Lord, the deeds for which he is to be praised, according to all the Lord has done for us—yes, the many good things he has done for Israel, according to his compassion and many kindnesses* (Isaiah 63:7).

### Look Within and Say I am Sorry – God, I am sorry . . .

We all mess up sometimes, and God wants us to come to Him and admit it. Was there a time recently that you were unkind? Let's talk to God about it. He can also help us say sorry to the person we were unkind to.

### Look Around and Thank Him – God, thank You for . . .

What are you thankful for today?
When we are thankful, it's hard for our hearts to feel mean or unkind. Thanking God helps us experience and live out His kindness.

### Look to Him and Ask – Fill me with Your **Kindness.**

*Be kind and compassionate to one another, forgiving each other, just as in Christ God forgave* _______________ (Ephesians 4:32).

GOD IS KIND

"I will tell of the kindnesses of the LORD, the deeds for which he is to be praised, according to all the LORD has done for us—yes, the many good things he has done for Israel, according to his compassion and many kindnesses."

Isaiah 63:7

# JOURNAL

## Prompt

Today, I am grateful for . . .

## Today, I am praying for . . .

# SESSION eight

**SESSION 8**
GOODNESS – GOD IS **GOOD**

**DATE** ______________________

## GETTING TO KNOW **YOU**

If you could plant a garden with anything in it, what would you grow?

What is the funniest thing that has ever happened to you?

What does it mean to be good?

Who is someone in your life who shows God's goodness through their actions?

See the **Appendix** for more questions.

## **TODAY** I'M FEELING . . .

excited

hopeful

worried

frustrated

creative

joyful

confused

**What are you curious about today?**

# GOD IS GOOD

Galatians 5:23 says:
*But the fruit of the Spirit is love, joy, peace, patience, kindness, goodness, faithfulness, gentleness and self-control.*

X marks the spot!

Imagine you have a map, and you are looking for hidden treasure. How do you find that treasure?

You look for clues, and all of those clues and signs lead you closer to the BIG treasure.

God's **goodness** is a lot like clues because we can find it everywhere we look, and these clues of His **goodness** lead us closer to Him!

What kind of clues do you see in your life? Have you ever seen a beautiful big waterfall or have you been to the beach?

God shows His **goodness** through His creation! And next time you see a rainbow, be reminded that God keeps His promises.

Who is someone that loves you so much? When we are loved by others, we experience God's love. I see God's **goodness** when I have food to eat, a warm comfy bed, and clothes to wear.

His **goodness** is everywhere. We just have to open our eyes to see it!

This week, I want you to look for clues of God's amazing **goodness**.

## Let's pray together!

### Look Up to Him in Praise – God, I love that You are **Good**.

*Give thanks to the Lord, for he is good; his love endures forever*
(1 Chronicles 16:34).

### Look Within and Say I am Sorry – God, I am sorry . . .

Has there been a time when it was hard to make good choices? We all sin, and God wants us to come to Him and admit it so that we can choose His way instead of our own.

### Look Around and Thank Him – God, thank You for . . .

What are you thankful for today?
When we are thankful, it's hard for our hearts to feel bad or discouraged. Thanking God helps us experience His goodness!

### Look to Him and Ask – God, help me trust in Your **Goodness** all the time.

______________, *Trust in the Lord with all your heart and lean not on your own understanding; in all your ways submit to him, and he will make* ______________ *paths straight*
(Proverbs 3:5–6).

GOD IS GOOD
ALL THE TIME

"Give thanks to the LORD, for he is good;
his love endures forever."

1 Chronicles 16:34

# JOURNAL
## Prompt

Today, I am grateful for . . .

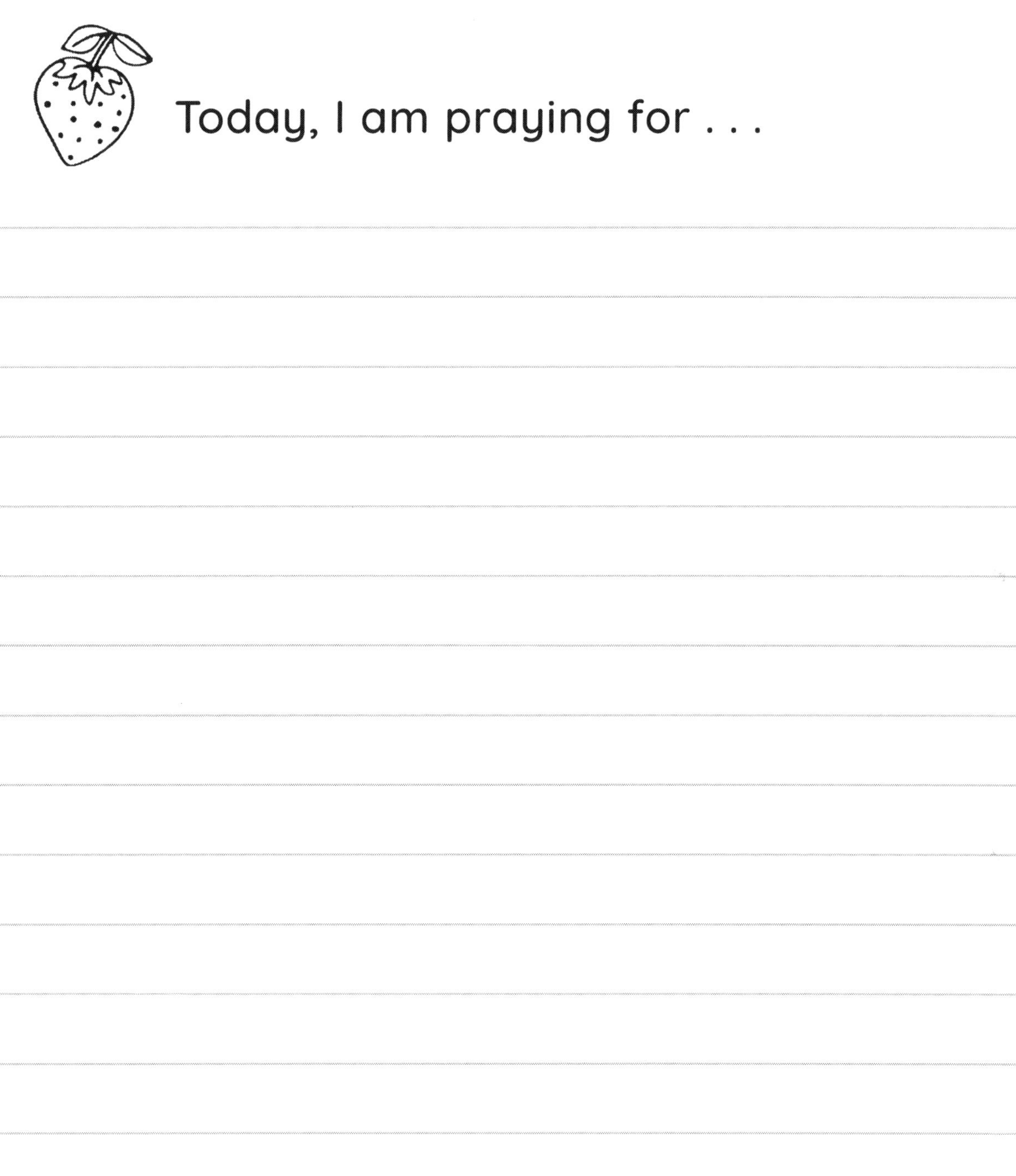

## Today, I am praying for . . .

# SESSION nine

**SESSION 9**

FAITHFULNESS - GOD IS **FAITHFUL** **DATE** ____________

# GETTING TO KNOW **YOU**

If you could make one rule that everyone in the world had to follow, what would it be?

Who is your closest friend(s)? Why are they your closest friend(s)?

How can you show faithfulness in your friendships?

Why is it important to be faithful, even when no one is watching?

See the **Appendix** for more questions.

# TODAY I'M FEELING . . .

excited

hopeful

worried

frustrated

creative

joyful

confused

**What are you curious about today?**

# GOD IS FAITHFUL

Galatians 5:23 says:
*But the fruit of the Spirit is love, joy, peace, patience, kindness, goodness, faithfulness, gentleness and self-control.*

Can you imagine being thrown into a lion's den?

I would be so scared! That's what happened to a guy named Daniel. Daniel loved God so much and was faithful in praying to Him every single day. The leaders of the land decided to make a decree that everyone was to pray only to the king. Despite this rule, Daniel kept praying to God and God alone.

He was thrown into a lion's den for breaking the law, but God faithfully protected him, and the next morning, Daniel was found unharmed by the lions. What's really amazing is that through Daniel's faithfulness to God and God's faithfulness to Daniel, the king acknowledged the power of God.

In this story, we see that God protected Daniel and that He is faithful. It encourages us to continually pray no matter what. We can pray knowing that God is faithful, and we can ask Him for help and for miracles. We pray with faith knowing He is capable of anything. He is faithful to us, even when we are unsure or don't have answers.

I think of God's faithfulness when it snows or storms. Snow is cold and winter feels like it will never end, but eventually the snow melts and then spring comes. What happens during the springtime? Flowers grow, trees turn green, and the sun comes out to warm us again.

God is faithful like that. Sometimes it snows and we don't know when it will melt, but we can trust that it will. And just like the springtime comes, so does God, because He is faithful to us.

## Let's pray together!

### Look Up to Him in Praise - God, I love that You are **Faithful.**

*Because of the LORD's great love we are not consumed, for his compassions never fail. They are new every morning; great is your faithfulness* (Lamentations 3:22–23).

### Look Within and Say I am Sorry - God, I am sorry . . .

We all sin, and God wants us to come to Him and admit it.

### Look Around and Thank Him - God, thank You for . . .

What are you thankful for today?
When we are thankful, it's hard for our hearts to feel alone or afraid. Thanking God helps us recognize His faithfulness.

### Look to Him and Ask - Help me to see Your **Faithfulness.**

*But the Lord is faithful, and he will strengthen* _____________ *and protect* _____________ *from the evil one* (2 Thessalonians 3:3).

GOD IS FAITHFUL

**"Because of the LORD's great love we are not consumed, for his compassions never fail. They are new every morning; great is your faithfulness."**

Lamentations 3:22-23

# JOURNAL
## Prompt

Today, I am grateful for . . .

Today, I am praying for . . .

# SESSION ten

**SESSION 10**
GENTLENESS – GOD IS **GENTLE** **DATE** ____________

# GETTING TO KNOW **YOU**

Would you rather go to space or explore the deep ocean?

Would you rather have the ability to read minds or control the weather?

What does "gentle" mean to you? Is there someone in your life who is gentle?

How can we show gentleness to others?

See the **Appendix** for more questions.

# TODAY
## I'M FEELING . . .

excited

hopeful

worried

frustrated

creative

joyful

confused

**What are you curious about today?**

# GOD IS GENTLE

Galatians 5:23 says:
*But the fruit of the Spirit is love, joy, peace, patience, kindness, goodness, faithfulness, gentleness and self-control.*

If you met Jesus face-to-face, what do you think He would say to you?

I can tell you what He wouldn't say: "Have you done all your chores? Have you been good?" Instead, He would pull you into His arms, and He would say, "I love you. I am so glad you are my friend," because He is **gentle** and kind.

The New Testament is full of so many stories of Jesus and His **gentleness**. He met so many people who messed up and who sinned, but He loved them, helped them and healed them. He didn't yell or shake His finger at them, but He cared for them with **gentle** kindness.

Jesus is The Good Shepherd and He always cares for His sheep. Jesus is God's Son, and the Bible says when we see Jesus we see His Father, and God is a loving, **gentle** Father.

He gives us what we need when we need it.

He is like a cool breeze on a hot day. He is like a warm hug when we're feeling sad. He is a light in the darkness when we feel afraid.

He is a loving and **gentle** God.

## Let's pray together!

**Look Up to Him in Praise** – God, I love that You are **Gentle.**

*"Come to me, all you who are weary and burdened, and I will give you rest. Take my yoke upon you and learn from me, for I am gentle and humble in heart, and you will find rest for your souls"* (Matthew 11:28–29).

**Look Within and Say I am Sorry** – God, I am sorry . . .

We all mess up, and God wants us to come to Him and admit it.

**Look Around and Thank Him** – God, thank You for . . .

What are you thankful for today?
When we are thankful, it's hard for our hearts to feel stressed or hurt. Thanking God helps us see His gentleness.

**Look to Him and Ask** – Help me be **Gentle** like You.

________________, *be completely humble and gentle; be patient, bearing with one another in love* (Ephesians 4:2).

GOD IS GENTLE

"Come to me, all you who are weary and burdened, and I will give you rest. Take my yoke upon you and learn from me, for I am gentle and humble in heart, and you will find rest for your souls."

Matthew 11:28-29

# JOURNAL
## Prompt

Today, I am grateful for . . .

Today, I am praying for . . .

# SESSION eleven

**SESSION 11**

SELF-CONTROL - GOD IS **IN CONTROL** **DATE** ____________

## GETTING TO KNOW **YOU**

What is your favorite memory from a vacation?

What is something that made you smile today?

Why is self-control important when you feel angry or frustrated?

How can you practice self-control when you really want something, but you know it's not the right time?

See the **Appendix** for more questions.

## TODAY I'M FEELING . . .

excited

hopeful

worried

frustrated

creative

joyful

confused

**What are you curious about today?**

# GOD IS IN CONTROL

Galatians 5:23 says:
*But the fruit of the Spirit is love, joy, peace, patience, kindness, goodness, faithfulness, gentleness and self-control.*

One day, Jesus and His friends were in a boat when a huge storm came. The waves were so big the men thought the boat would sink. They were pretty scared.

Do you know what Jesus was doing during this storm? He was asleep! His disciples woke Him up, saying, "Lord, save us! We're going to drown!" Jesus stood up and told the storm to stop, and it did! The water became calm again, and the disciples got to witness that Jesus is truly in control of everything. (Matthew 8:23–27)

There are a lot of things that we can't control. Sometimes school can be hard, or our siblings can make us mad. Sometimes we might feel worried or tired or afraid. Remember, God is in control and will help us through every homework assignment, test, relationship, and difficult situation.

We can't control how our friends treat us or what our siblings do, but we *can* control what we say. We can pray and ask God to help us be kind. He's always there to guide us.

God is working everything out for our good. He is in control of the wind and the waves, and when we say yes to Him, we also give Him control of our lives. His way is so much better!

## Let's pray together!

**Look Up to Him in Praise –** God, I love that You are **in Control.**

*He is before all things, and in him all things hold together* (Colossians 1:17).

**Look Within and Say I am Sorry –** God, I am sorry . . .

We all mess up, and God wants us to come to Him and admit it.

**Look Around and Thank Him –** God, thank You for . . .

What are you thankful for today? When we are thankful, it's hard for our hearts to feel out of control. Thanking God helps us experience the safety of His control in our lives.

**Look to Him and Ask –** Help me have **Self-Control** with myself and others.

*For God gave ________________ a spirit not of fear but of power and love and self-control* (2 Timothy 1:7, ESV).

GOD IS IN CONTROL

"He is before all things, and in him all things hold together."
Colossians 1:17

# JOURNAL

Prompt

Today, I am grateful for . . .

## Today, I am praying for . . .

# SESSION twelve

**SESSION 12**
GO **BEAR FRUIT**

**DATE** ______________

# GETTING TO KNOW **YOU**

Would you rather be a famous inventor or a famous artist? What would you design?

What is the most interesting thing you've learned this week?

How do you stay connected to Jesus every day?

What does the Fruit of the Spirit mean to you? Which one do you feel is the most important?

See the **Appendix** for more questions.

# **TODAY** I'M FEELING . . .

excited

hopeful

worried

frustrated

creative

joyful

confused

**What are you curious about today?**

# GO BEAR FRUIT

Galatians 5:23 says:
*But the fruit of the Spirit is love, joy, peace, patience, kindness, goodness, faithfulness, gentleness and self-control.*

Have you ever looked at a tree that has lots of branches, leaves, flowers or maybe even fruit? To grow big and strong, those branches must stay connected to the tree.

What happens if they aren't connected to the tree and break off? Will they still produce leaves, flowers or fruit?

In the same way, John 15:4–5 tells us, just like a branch, we must stay connected to Jesus so that we may bear fruit like love, joy, peace, patience, kindness, goodness, faithfulness, gentleness and self-control.

(Have you memorized all of those yet? I bet you can!)

How can you "bear fruit" every day? Let's think of some ideas of how you can show love, be patient, be gentle or practice self-control.

Remember, the only way we can do that well is to stay close to Jesus, to pray to Him throughout the day and to read God's Word.

Check out the appendix section for more verses, questions and activities for guidance as your mentee learns what it looks like to stay close to Jesus.

## Let's pray together!

**Look Up to Him in Praise –** God, I love that you help me **bear fruit.**

*"I am the vine; you are the branches. If you remain in me and I in you, you will bear much fruit; apart from me you can do nothing"* (John 15:5).

**Look Within and Say I am Sorry –** God, I am sorry . . .

We all sin, and God wants us to come to Him and admit it.

**Look Around and Thank Him –** God, thank You for . . .

What are you thankful for today? When we are thankful, it's hard for our hearts to feel empty or useless. Thanking God helps us experience all the Fruit of His Spirit!

**Look to Him and Ask –** God, help me remain in You.

Help your mentee understand what it means to be close to Jesus. This can be a topic you continue to discuss. Talk about the power of reading God's Word and praying throughout our day asking the Lord for His wisdom and help!

*Remain in me, as I also remain in ____________. No branch can bear fruit by itself; it must remain in the vine. Neither can ____________ bear fruit unless you remain in me* (John 15:4).

GOD IS THE VINE

"I am the vine; you are the branches. If you remain in me and I in you, you will bear much fruit; apart from me you can do nothing."

John 15:5

# JOURNAL
## Prompt

Today, I am grateful for . . .

## Today, I am praying for . . .

# APPENDIX

## A. Scripture
additional/memorize

## B. Dive Deeper
with more questions for each session

## C. Getting to Know You
questions

## D. Activity
recommendations

## E. Leading a Mentee
to Christ

## F. Emotion Wheel
How are you feeling today?

## APPENDIX

Hey Mentor!

This appendix is for you so that you may receive support to help a younger mentee or to dive deeper and offer extensions for older mentees. We hope this is a great resource for you as you answer (and ask) big questions or engage in more activities.

---

# A. SCRIPTURE

### Additional Scripture for each session

We have provided more Scripture that talks about God's love, joy, peace, patience, kindness, goodness, faithfulness, gentleness and self-control. Encourage your mentee to star these verses in their Bible, to memorize or to make their own list on a notecard for a Bible bookmark or in the journal portion of the guide. This is a great way to teach your mentee to cross-reference verses and to dive deeper in each session.

### 1. Holy Spirit

*But you will receive power when the Holy Spirit comes on you; and you will be my witnesses in Jerusalem, and in all Judea and Samaria, and to the ends of the earth* (Acts 1:8).

*For those who are led by the Spirit of God are the children of God* (Romans 8:14).

*Do you not know that your bodies are temples of the Holy Spirit, who is in you, whom you have received from God? You are not your own* (1 Corinthians 6:19).

*And you also were included in Christ when you heard the message of truth, the gospel of your salvation. When you believed, you were marked in him with a seal, the promised Holy Spirit, who is a deposit guaranteeing our inheritance until the redemption of those who are God's possession—to the praise of his glory* (Ephesians 1:13–14).

*But when he, the Spirit of truth, comes, he will guide you into all the truth. He will not speak on his own; he will speak only what he hears, and he will tell you what is yet to come* (John 16:13).

*So I say, walk by the Spirit, and you will not gratify the desires of the flesh* (Galatians 5:16).

## 2. God is with me

*When you pass through the waters, I will be with you; and when you pass through the rivers, they will not sweep over you. When you walk through the fire, you will not be burned; the flames will not set you ablaze* (Isaiah 43:2).

*For where two or three gather in my name, there am I with them* (Matthew 18:20).

*Have I not commanded you? Be strong and courageous. Do not be afraid; do not be discouraged, for the LORD your God will be with you wherever you go* (Joshua 1:9).

*The LORD is near to all who call on him, to all who call on him in truth* (Psalm 145:18).

*And surely I am with you always, to the very end of the age* (Matthew 28:20b).

## 3. Love

*For God so loved the world that he gave his one and only Son, that whoever believes in him shall not perish but have eternal life* (John 3:16).

*But God demonstrates his own love for us in this: While we were still sinners, Christ died for us* (Romans 5:8).

*Dear friends, let us love one another, for love comes from God. Everyone who loves has been born of God and knows God* (1 John 4:7).

*Whoever does not love does not know God, because God is love* (1 John 4:8).

*This is how God showed his love among us: He sent his one and only Son into the world that we might live through him* (1 John 4:9).

*And so we know and rely on the love God has for us. God is love. Whoever lives in love lives in God, and God in them* (1 John 4:16).

*But you, Lord, are a compassionate and gracious God, slow to anger, abounding in love and faithfulness* (Psalm 86:15).

*The Lord your God is with you, the Mighty Warrior who saves. He will take great delight in you; in his love he will no longer rebuke you, but will rejoice over you with singing* (Zephaniah 3:17).

## 4. Joy

*You make known to me the path of life; you will fill me with joy in your presence, with eternal pleasures at your right hand* (Psalm 16:11).

*Weeping may stay for the night, but rejoicing comes in the morning* (Psalm 30:5b).

*Taste and see that the Lord is good; blessed is the one who takes refuge in him* (Psalm 34:8).

*When anxiety was great within me, your consolation brought me joy* (Psalm 94:19).

*Do not grieve, for the joy of the Lord is your strength* (Nehemiah 8:10b).

## 5. Peace

*You will keep in perfect peace those whose minds are steadfast, because they trust in you* (Isaiah 26:3).

*May the God of hope fill you with all joy and peace as you trust in him, so that you may overflow with hope by the power of the Holy Spirit* (Romans 15:13).

*Peace I leave with you; my peace I give you. I do not give to you as the world gives. Do not let your hearts be troubled and do not be afraid* (John 14:27).

*And the peace of God, which transcends all understanding, will guard your hearts and your minds in Christ Jesus* (Philippians 4:7).

## 6. Patience

*But you, Lord, are a compassionate and gracious God, slow to anger, abounding in love and faithfulness* (Psalm 86:15).

*The LORD is slow to anger but great in power; the LORD will not leave the guilty unpunished* (Nahum 1:3a).

*The Lord is not slow in keeping his promise, as some understand slowness. Instead he is patient with you, not wanting anyone to perish, but everyone to come to repentance* (2 Peter 3:9).

*But for that very reason I was shown mercy so that in me, the worst of sinners, Christ Jesus might display his immense patience as an example for those who would believe in him and receive eternal life* (1 Timothy 1:16).

*Or do you show contempt for the riches of his kindness, forbearance, and patience, not realizing that God's kindness is intended to lead you to repentance?* (Romans 2:4)

## 7. Kindness

*The LORD is good to all; he has compassion on all he has made* (Psalm 145:9).

*The LORD is righteous in all his ways and kind in all his works* (Psalm 145:17, ESV).

*Return to the LORD your God, for he is gracious and compassionate, slow to anger and abounding in love; and he relents from sending calamity* (Joel 2:13b).

*The Lord appeared to us in the past, saying: "I have loved you with an everlasting love; I have drawn you with unfailing kindness"* (Jeremiah 31:3).

*When Jesus landed and saw a large crowd, he had compassion on them and healed their sick* (Matthew 14:14).

## 8. Goodness

*Taste and see that the LORD is good; blessed is the one who takes refuge in him* (Psalm 34:8).

*For the Lord is good and his love endures forever; his faithfulness continues through all generations* (Psalm 100:5).

*The Lord is good, a refuge in times of trouble. He cares for those who trust in him* (Nahum 1:7).

*I remain confident of this: I will see the goodness of the Lord in the land of the living* (Psalm 27:13).

*The earth is full of the goodness of the Lord* (Psalm 33:5b, NASB).

*Surely your goodness and love will follow me all the days of my life, and I will dwell in the house of the Lord forever* (Psalm 23:6).

## 9. Faithfulness

*The Lord is trustworthy in all he promises and faithful in all he does* (Psalm 145:13b).

*Know therefore that the Lord your God is God; he is the faithful God, keeping his covenant of love to a thousand generations of those who love him and keep his commandments* (Deuteronomy 7:9).

*Your faithfulness continues through all generations; you established the earth, and it endures* (Psalm 119:90).

*If we are faithless, he remains faithful, for he cannot disown himself* (2 Timothy 2:13).

*The one who calls you is faithful, and he will do it* (1 Thessalonians 5:24).

*Let us hold unswervingly to the hope we profess, for he who promised is faithful* (Hebrews 10:23).

## 10. Gentleness

*He tends his flock like a shepherd: he gathers the lambs in his arms and carries them close to his heart; he gently leads those that have young* (Isaiah 40:11).

*You have given me the shield of your salvation, and your right hand supported me, and your gentleness made me great* (Psalm 18:35, ESV).

*Let your gentleness be evident to all. The Lord is near* (Philippians 4:5).

*But we were gentle among you, like a nursing mother taking care of her own children* (1 Thessalonians 2:7, ESV).

**11. Self-Control**

*The Lord is upright; he is my Rock, and there is no wickedness in him* (Psalm 92:15).

*The heart of man plans his way, but the Lord establishes his steps* (Proverbs 16:9, ESV).

*The Lord has established his throne in the heavens, and his kingdom rules over all* (Psalm 103:19, ESV).

*"For I know the plans I have for you," declares the Lord, "plans to prosper you and not to harm you, plans to give you hope and a future"* (Jeremiah 29:11).

*The Lord is my shepherd; I have all that I need. He lets me rest in green meadows; he leads me beside peaceful streams. He renews my strength. He guides me along right paths, bringing honor to his name* (Psalm 23:1–3, NLT).

*Like a city whose walls are broken through is a person who lacks self-control* (Proverbs 25:28).

*Better a patient person than a warrior, one with self-control than one who takes a city* (Proverbs 16:32).

**12. Abiding in Christ and Bearing Fruit**

*"I am the true grapevine, and my father is the gardener. He cuts off every branch of mine that doesn't produce fruit, and he prunes the branches that do bear fruit so they will produce even more. You have already been pruned and purified by the message I have given you"* (John 15:1-3, NLT).

*"But if you remain in me and my words remain in you, you may ask me for anything you want, and it will be granted! When you produce much fruit, you are my true disciples. This brings great glory to my Father"* (John 15:7-8, NLT).

*"I have loved you even as the Father has loved me. Remain in my love. When you obey my commandments, you remain in my love, just as I obey my Father's commandments and remain in his love. I have told you these things so that you will be filled with my joy. Yes, your joy will overflow!"* (John 15:9-11, NLT)

*"You didn't choose me. I chose you. I appointed you to go and produce lasting fruit, so that the Father will give you whatever you ask for, using my name"* (John 15:16, NLT).

**Memorize Scripture**

*I have hidden your word in my heart, that I might not sin against you. I praise you, O Lord; teach me your decrees* (Psalm 119:11–12).

When God's Word is stored in our hearts, it becomes truth in our lives and a guiding lamp for our feet. Scripture memorized comes back to us when we are nervous, afraid, when we worship and pray, and when we seek wisdom from the Lord. The Holy Spirit is our reminder and reminds us of Scripture!

Encourage your mentee to memorize Scripture. Maybe start small with one verse a week. Help them understand that memorizing Scripture isn't just about remembering words; it's about keeping God's truth close so it can guide us every day.

Use creative methods like songs, games, or even friendly challenges to make the process fun and engaging. They can hang their coloring page to help them, write the verse with different color markers on note cards or act it out.

Maybe offer a little reward!

Most importantly, tell them how memorizing Scripture has impacted your own life or how it is something you want to do with them.

# B. DIVE DEEPER
## With More Questions For Each Session

**Session 1 - Holy Spirit**

If someone were to ask you, "What is the Holy Spirit?" what would you tell them?
Was there a time in your life that you felt the Holy Spirit speaking or nudging you in some way?
What questions do you have about the Holy Spirit?

**Session 2 - God is with Me**

Can you remember a time you didn't feel very brave? What did you do?
God is always with us. In what ways do you feel His presence?
Is there something that you worry about? What will you do when you start to worry or fear?

**Session 3 - God is Love**

How do you think God's love is different from the love we experience from our family and friends?
Can you think of a time when you felt God's love in your life? What happened, and how did it make you feel?
Why do you think it's important for us to show love to others, just like God shows love to us?

**Session 4 - God is Joy**

What do you think it means when the Bible says that God finds joy in us?
What are some small things you can do every day to bring more joy into your life and the lives of others?
Why do you think it's important to have joy in our hearts?

**Session 5 - God is Peace**

Why is it important to have peace in our hearts and minds?
Why do you think it's important to trust in God's peace when we are worried or scared?
How can we remind ourselves of God's peace in difficult moments?

**Session 6 - God is Patient**

Do you feel stronger after you have been patient?
How do you think God helps us be patient when we pray and trust Him?
How does God's patience help you grow closer to Him?

### Session 7 - God is Kind

What are some ways you've seen or felt God's kindness in your life, and how did it make you feel?
When is it hard to be kind?
How do you think kindness can change someone's day or even their life?

### Session 8 - God is Good

Why do you think it's important to remember that God is always good, even when things don't go as we planned?
What kind of clues do you see of God's goodness?
How can you show God's goodness to others through your actions and words?

### Session 9 - God is Faithful

What are some ways you can show faithfulness in your everyday life?
How can remembering God's faithfulness in the past help you stay hopeful and confident in the future? Can you think of some ways to remind yourself of this?
Why is it important to trust that God will be faithful, even when we don't see things working out the way we hoped?

### Session 10 - God is Gentle

What does it mean to you that God is gentle, and how do you think His gentleness can make a difference in our lives?
Do you find it easy or difficult to be gentle? Why?
When are there times that it's really important to be gentle? What could happen if you aren't?

### Session 11 - God is in control

What does it mean to have self-control? What are some good examples of good self-control?
Why do you think it can be challenging to control our actions or feelings sometimes, and how can remembering God's help or guidance make it easier?
How can practicing self-control in small things, like managing your time or handling emotions, help you in bigger situations? Can you give an example?

### Session 12 - Go Bear Fruit

What are some ways that you remain close to Christ?
Is there something you want to work on together (read the Bible, pray, memorize verses, talk together)?
Why is it important to bear fruit?

# C. GET TO KNOW YOU QUESTIONS

**Conversation Starters | Would You Rather . . . ?**

Would you rather be able to fly or be invisible?
Would you rather have a pet dinosaur or a pet dragon?
Would you rather live in a castle or on a spaceship?
Would you rather live in a cloud in the sky or an underwater city?
Would you rather eat ice cream for every meal or never eat ice cream again?
Would you rather be able to talk to animals or speak every language in the world?
Would you rather have the ability to time travel or the ability to teleport anywhere instantly?
Would you rather have a superpower to control the weather or to control time?
Would you rather always have to hop on one foot or always have to crawl on all fours?
Would you rather have a room filled with toys or a room filled with books?
Would you rather be as small as an ant or as big as a giant?
Would you rather live in a treehouse or live in a houseboat?
Would you rather be friends with a talking dolphin or a talking monkey?
Would you rather have super strength or super speed?
Would you rather have your dream job when you grow up or your dream house when you grow up?
Would you rather be able to make your toys come to life or be able to turn into any toy you want?
Would you rather have the ability to make people laugh whenever you want or be able to make people stop crying whenever you want?
Would you rather always talk in rhymes or sing everything you say?
Would you rather have the power to make plants grow instantly or to make it rain whenever you want?
Would you rather have a tree that grows your favorite fruit or a fountain that gives you your favorite drink?

**Conversation Starters | (Continued)**

What is your favorite book or story?
What is your favorite thing to do on the weekends?
If you could visit any place in the world, where would you go?
If you could meet any cartoon character, who would it be?
If you could have any animal as a pet, real or imaginary, what would it be and why?
If you could have any job in the world for a day, what would you choose and what would you do?
If you could invent something, what would it be?
If you could be any character from a movie or book, who would you be?
What is your favorite holiday and why?
What's the best adventure you've ever been on?
What is the best gift you have ever received?
What is something that made you smile today?
Who is your best friend and what do you like to do together?
What is your favorite family tradition?
What is your favorite thing to do with your parents?
What is something nice you did for someone recently?
If you could have any animal as a pet, which one would you choose and why?
What is something you are really good at?
What is the nicest thing someone has ever done for you?
What is your favorite way to help out at home?
What is your favorite song to sing or listen to?
What is your favorite way to spend a rainy day?
What is something new you learned recently?
What is your favorite way to show someone you care?
What is your favorite thing to do with your friends?
If you could instantly learn any skill or talent, what would it be and what would you use it for?
If you could have a superpower to help others, what would it be?
What is your favorite bedtime story or book?
What is something that always makes you laugh?
If you could turn any activity into an Olympic sport, what would you choose and why?

# D. ACTIVITY RECOMMENDATIONS

**1. Kindness Cards**
Fruit of the Spirit: Kindness
Materials Needed: Paper, markers or crayons

Instructions:
1. Each of you takes a piece of paper and some markers or crayons.
2. Create a card for someone you know (a friend, family member, or teacher).
3. Decorate the card and write a kind message inside.
4. Exchange your cards with each other to check and appreciate the kind words.
5. Give your card to the person you made it for and see how it brightens their day!

**2. Patience Partner Puzzle**
Fruit of the Spirit: Patience
Materials Needed: A simple jigsaw puzzle (20–30 pieces)

Instructions:
1. Work together to complete the jigsaw puzzle.
2. Take turns placing one piece at a time.
3. If you get stuck, wait patiently and encourage each other until you find the right piece.
4. Celebrate when you finish the puzzle together!

**3. Fruit of the Spirit Scavenger Hunt**
Fruit of the Spirit: Joy
Materials Needed: A list of simple items to find (e.g., a red leaf, a smooth rock, a piece of string)

Instructions:
1. Create a list of items to find around your house or yard.
2. Work with your partner to find each item on the list.
3. Share a joyful moment and high-five each time you find an item.
4. Once all items are found, discuss which one made you the happiest and why.

**4. Giving Compliments**
Fruit of the Spirit: Goodness
Materials Needed: None

Instructions:
1. Sit across from your partner.
2. Take turns giving each other genuine compliments.
3. Try to give at least three compliments each.
4. Discuss how receiving and giving compliments makes you feel.

**5. Helping Hands**
Fruit of the Spirit: Love
Materials Needed: None

Instructions:
1. Each of you think of one way to help the other person.
2. Perform the act of kindness (e.g., help with homework, tidy up toys, share a snack).
3. Talk about how helping each other shows love and how it made you feel.
4. Make a promise to continue helping each other regularly.

These activities are designed to be engaging, simple, and meaningful, reinforcing the values of the Fruit of the Spirit.

**6. The Fruit ABCs**
It's time to test your fruit knowledge! Can you name a fruit that starts with each letter of the alphabet?
Materials Needed: A pen, paper, coloring supplies (optional)

Instructions:
1. Begin with the letter "A" and write down (or draw) a fruit that starts with that letter. For example, "A is for Apple."
2. Continue going through the entire alphabet, either writing or drawing out each fruit. See if you can get all the way to Z!

Mix it up:
After you complete the full alphabet, answer these questions:
*What is a fruit that you have never tried?*
*What is your favorite fruit?*
*How do fruits grow? Do all fruits grow the same way?*

**7. Kindness Chain**
Fruit of the Spirit: Kindness
Materials Needed: Strips of colorful paper, markers, tape or glue

Instructions:

1. Write one kind act on each strip of paper (e.g., "Help a friend," "Share a toy," "Say something nice").
2. Form a paper chain by linking the strips together using tape or glue.
3. Each day, remove one link from the chain and perform the kind act written on it.
4. Watch the chain grow smaller as your kindness grows!

**8. Peaceful Painting**
Fruit of the Spirit: Peace
Materials Needed: Paper, paint, brushes, calming music

Instructions:

1. Play some calming music in the background.
2. Encourage the children to paint something that makes them feel peaceful, like a serene landscape or a favorite quiet place.
3. After painting, discuss how creating art in a calm environment can help us feel peaceful inside.
4. Display the paintings as a reminder to seek peace in daily life.

**9. Self-Control Relay**
Fruit of the Spirit: Self-Control
Materials Needed: Small objects like spoons, balls, or cups

Instructions:

1. Set up a relay course with small obstacles.
2. Each child must carry a small object (e.g., a spoon with a ball on it) through the course without dropping it.
3. If the object drops, the child must start over, practicing self-control to move carefully.
4. Celebrate the completion of the relay with a discussion about how self-control helps us in difficult situations.

**10. Gentle Words Storytime**
Fruit of the Spirit: Gentleness
Materials Needed: A favorite storybook

Instructions:

1. Read a story aloud that includes characters showing gentleness (e.g., helping someone, speaking kindly).
2. Pause during the story to discuss how the characters' gentle actions made a difference.

3. After the story, encourage the children to share a time when they used gentle words or actions with someone else.

**11. Faithfulness Garden**
Fruit of the Spirit: Faithfulness
Materials Needed: Small flower pots, soil, seeds, watering can

Instructions:
1. Plant seeds in the small pots and water them together.
2. Talk about how taking care of the plants every day is like being faithful in our actions.
3. As the plants grow, relate it to how our faithfulness helps us grow in other areas of life.
4. Encourage the child to take responsibility for watering and caring for their plants regularly.

**12. Joyful Jumps**
Fruit of the Spirit: Joy
Materials Needed: Chalk, jump rope, or a simple hopscotch grid

Instructions:
1. Draw a hopscotch grid or set up a jump rope area.
2. Each time a child lands on a square or completes a jump, they must shout out something that brings them joy.
3. Continue the game until everyone has shared several joyful moments.
4. Discuss how sharing joy with others can make us even happier.

**13. Peaceful Listening**
Fruit of the Spirit: Peace
Materials Needed: Calming music, a comfortable space to sit

Instructions:
1. Gather the child in a comfortable, quiet space.
2. Play calming music and encourage the child to close their eyes and listen quietly.
3. After a few minutes, ask them to share how the music made them feel and discuss how finding moments of peace can help us feel calm and centered throughout the day.

**14. Patience Planting**
Fruit of the Spirit: Patience
Materials Needed: Slow-growing plant seeds (e.g., sunflowers), pots, soil

Instructions:
1. Plant seeds in small pots and talk about how it takes time and patience for the seeds to grow.
2. Encourage the children to water their plants regularly and observe the slow growth.
3. Discuss how practicing patience in life is similar to waiting for a plant to grow—good things take time!

**15. Gentle Garden Stretching**
Fruit of the Spirit: Gentleness
Materials Needed: A soft surface like a mat or grassy area

Instructions:
1. Gather the children in a calm outdoor or indoor space.
2. Lead them through a series of gentle stretching poses, emphasizing slow and gentle movements.
3. As they move through each pose, talk about how gentleness isn't just about how we treat others, but also how we care for ourselves.
4. After the session, discuss how practicing gentleness with our bodies helps us feel calm and strong.

**16. Goodness Goals**
Fruit of the Spirit: Goodness
Materials Needed: Paper, markers

Instructions:
1. Have the children think of one good thing they can do each day for the next week.
2. Ask them to write or draw their goal on a piece of paper.
3. Each day, have them reflect on their progress and discuss how doing good makes them feel and how it affects others.
4. At the end of the week, celebrate their efforts to practice goodness.

**17. Love Letters**
Fruit of the Spirit: Love
Materials Needed: Paper, markers, envelopes

Instructions:
1. Have each child write a letter to someone they love, expressing their feelings and appreciation.
2. Decorate the letters with drawings or stickers.
3. Seal the letters in envelopes and discuss how sharing love through words

can make a big impact.
4. Encourage the children to give the letter to the person they wrote it for.

**18. Kindness Coin Flip**
Fruit of the Spirit: Kindness
Materials Needed: A coin

Instructions:
1. The mentor and mentee take turns flipping a coin.
2. Each time the coin lands on heads, the mentor gives an example of a kind act they've done or seen recently. If it lands on tails, the mentee shares their example.
3. After a few rounds, discuss how simple acts of kindness can make a big difference in someone's day and brainstorm ways to practice kindness in their daily lives.
4. Reflect on how kindness, like the flip of a coin, can seem small but has the power to change outcomes.

**19. Joy Jar**
Fruit of the Spirit: Joy
Materials Needed: A jar, slips of paper, pens

Instructions:
1. Each day, have the children write something that brought them joy.
2. Place the slips of paper into the jar.
3. At the end of the week, open the jar and read all the joyful moments together.
4. Discuss how focusing on joy can help us feel happy and thankful.

**20. Faithfulness Friendship Bracelets**
Fruit of the Spirit: Faithfulness
Materials Needed: Colorful beads, string

Instructions:
1. Provide the child with beads and string to make a friendship bracelet.
2. As they create the bracelet, talk about how being a good friend means being faithful and dependable.
3. Encourage them to give the bracelet to a friend as a reminder of their faithful friendship.
4. Discuss how faithfulness in friendships is important, just like being faithful in other parts of life.

# E. LEADING A MENTEE TO CHRIST

### ABC's of Accepting Christ

A - **Admit** that you are a sinner and need a Savior, and that you are willing to turn away from your sins and be sorry for your sins.

*For all have sinned and fall short of the glory of God* (Romans 3:23).

B - **Believe** that Jesus is the Son of God and that He died and rose again to pay for your sins.

*For God so loved the world that he gave his only Son, that whoever believes in him shall not perish but have eternal life* (John 3:16).

C - **Confess** that Jesus Christ is your Lord and Savior and that you want to trust and follow Him.

*If you confess with your mouth that Jesus is Lord and believe in your heart that God raised him from the dead, you will be saved. For with the heart one believes and is justified, and with the mouth one confesses and is saved* (Romans 10:9–10, ESV).

We offer this prayer for you to guide your mentee if they want to accept Christ as their Savior:

*God, I am a sinner and I need you.*
*I am sorry and ask for your forgiveness. (Admit)*

*I believe that Jesus Christ is Your Son, that He died to rescue me and that You raised Him to life. (Believe)*

*Jesus, I trust You fully, and from this day on, I invite You to have control of my life and to be my guide and my helper through Your Holy Spirit that You have given me.*

*I want to follow You and be your disciple. (Confess)*

*I love You. Thank You for saving me so that I can live with You forever!*
*I pray this in the name of Jesus.*

*Amen.*

# F. EMOTION WHEEL

## How are you feeling today?

worried
hopeful
joyful
creative
bored
confused
excited
frustrated

# TELL ME MORE

At **MORE Mentoring**, our vision is to see Jesus fully experienced in mentoring relationships, and our mission is mobilizing mentors to impact lives through prayer-focused mentoring. We empower and equip mentors with tools, training, and an online community.

Help us reach our goal of **ONE MILLION** mentors by sharing this ministry with others. Growing the local church by encouraging all people to be engaged in mentoring—whether as a mentee, a mentor, or a mobilizer—is something we care deeply about. We know the world will be a better place as mentors rise up and step into their God-given callings to invest in the lives of others.

We would love to hear how mentoring has impacted your life. Please reach out to **info@morementoring.org** and share your story with us!

---

## TOOLS

Get equipped with our mentoring guides—the best tools to have on the journey of mentoring.

## TRAINING

Watch videos that will transform your mentoring journey. We're here to help you take that first step.

## COMMUNITY

Come together and see the vision multiplied. Join our community to Belong + Become.

**LEARN MORE**

---

# IF YOU WANT MORE

## LEARN MORE

Teens are at a critical stage of life, exploring their identity and making important decisions, but many feel alone and hopeless. *Together - Walk With Me* is a 12-session teen mentoring guide offering one-on-one support, spiritual guidance, icebreakers, activities, reflective questions, and prayer prompts to help mentors and teens grow closer to God and each other. Our hope is for your teen to leave transformed, encouraged, and more in love with Jesus.

"When I met with my mentee for the first time and asked what her expectations were for our relationship, she emphatically responded, 'I just want real.' Her words captured the longing of her generation for authentic, vulnerable relationships. They crave someone who will walk with them, offering hope, truth, and wisdom, while allowing them to be real and experience the power of genuine connection. Come join me on this mentoring adventure that might not only change your life, but also transform families, communities, churches, and the world."

**Nancy Lindgren**
**Founder and CEO, MORE Mentoring**

# SOCIALLY MORE

facebook.com/morementoring

MORE Mentoring

instagram.com/morementoring

MORE Mentoring

We would love to hear your stories of how God has worked in your life through these mentoring guides. Please email us at:

info@morementoring.org
**morementoring.org**

Made in the USA
Monee, IL
02 May 2025

16726617R00074